The Missing Angle
by Karine Leno Ancellin

The Missing Angle

Copyright © 2019 by Karine Leno Ancellin
All rights reserved. No part of this publication may be reproduced, distributed, or transmitted in any form or by any means, including photocopying, recording, or other electronic or mechanical methods, without the prior written permission of the publisher, except in the case of brief quotations embodied in critical reviews and certain other noncommercial uses permitted by copyright law.

First Printing, 2019
Printing information available on the last page.

ISBN (sc) 978-1-9992272-8-9
ISBN (e) 978-1-9992272-9-6

Editor: Beth Huston
Photography: Angela Lyras & Myrsini Gana
Riza Publishing Press
Ottawa, ON, Canada
www.rizapress.com

interior photography
by Myrsini Gana

cover photography
by Angela Lyras

Table of Contents

Foreword by Orfeas Apergis.. 7
Preface by John Murray.. 9

PART I: ETCHINGS
Interview with the Moon.. 13
Nude with Calla Lily, Diego Rivera.................................... 15
Rattleback Spin.. 17
Non-Aligned Love... 19
Art Tandem... 21
Midwifing the Poem... 23

PART II: VIRTUAL YEARNINGS
Skype Tear... 27
iCloud... 29
buy-ebay... 31
Mood Button.. 35
Gmail Novel.. 37
Late in Love.. 39
Complex Vortex... 41
Siphoned... 43
Soft Stone.. 45
Tangible Melancholy.. 47
Scopophilia... 49
Insomnia V.. 51
Sinister Semester.. 53
From Ares to Eros.. 55

PART III: ACCENTS OF MYTHS
Odysseas.. 61
Free Fall... 65
Exile in Frantic Folly... 69
Pireas Welcome... 71
Racked Refugees... 75
Athena's Blaze... 77
On the Wall Stood a Picture.. 81
Fluid Dawn... 83
In-divi-dual.. 85
Pathetic Pragmatism... 87

PART IV: EPILOGUE
Mooted.. 91
A Note on Coffee Grinds... 95

Afterword by Lee Slonimsky.. 97

Foreword
by Orfeas Apergis

"Greece handed me what I didn't know I was missing, everything I had been entitled to, and bereft of, a mythology to face the travails of the day, a home with a poetic room of my own," says Karine Ancellin in her "Epilogue" to this set of poems, a collection which places her much-divided and multifarious self in the midst of the travails of globalisation. This is the quietly meandering but always agonizing cry of a modern "citizen of the world," at home in New York or Paris, or Athens, or the Greek isles, or Subsaharan Africa and the Tuareg. "I know of him, and of his sorrows," she dolefully yet somehow optimistically admits, speaking of Ulysses. So here is someone who arrives in Greece as a "xenos", a foreigner, but manages to "stay and nest, grow 'roots and safety', her vital delicacies." And indeed, there is much delicate vitality to Ancellin's poetic work, so much so that her record of the travails of globalisation—where "racked refugees" "desperately seek dignity at the Greek Port of Pireas, [and] hunger tenses, legs rush by, as the magnitude, in despair, is engulfing foreign goodwill"—this unyielding record remains, almost curiously, doggedly upbeat, if not downright optimistic. How does she manage this? She does it through poetry; putting her thoughtful feelings and feeling thoughts down on paper, singing of her love across the ocean and her "communing in love" through the very imperfect conduit of skype, where her "heart stoops to the moment—the beats throbbing too loud for this pixelated slowness," she finds a quasi-miraculous 'trope' of feeling her way through the madness that our world currently is. This is a richly rewarding collection—complete with latter-day, disjointed yet insistent rhymes—by a master-craftswoman wielding the very potent weapon that International English has become. Throughout, Injustice and Love, "Ares and Eros" as she puts it, co-exist in a frenzied dance of opposing antinomies, and Ancellin is torn between the rival warring factions of her life as she globe-trots, inviting us to take a seat and enjoy her "awry, acerbic and sensitive critique" of a ride—"as if [her] answers mocked the exercise." Read this and revel in its "commitment to the ecstasy and elegance of non-alignment and no chosen stance."

Orfeas Apergis is a contemporary poet, author of 'Υ' and 'Η γλώσσα τους' poetry collections.

Preface
by John Murray, London, November 2019

My lover left a stone in my hand

Drumming the beach with her long legs
veins on marble, lines on limestone
fine faint frontiers playing on her translucent flesh
    - from "Soft Stone" by Karine Ancellin

In the world of Classical Sanskrit poetry, there were two different schools of thought when it came to analysing how a poem touched the reader. The Rasikas believed that real poetry produced a profound and sublime aesthetic rapture, called 'rasa', meaning literally 'taste', but equivalent to the bliss of spiritual transcendence (interestingly that legendary stickler of an author, Vladimir Nabokov, believed in a similar aesthetic when it came to great fiction). The opposing school, the Dhvanikas, argued that a real poet used words so that they produced an ineffable 'echo' or dhvani, and the echo resonated in such a way that it subtly and mysteriously suggested what was sublime, rather than mechanically elaborating the desired aesthetic effect.

I think the Dhvanikas would have very much liked Karine's poem above. The first line about the stone is simplicity itself, but perhaps the assonance of 'tn' and 'nd' in 'stone' and 'hand' is what effectively opens up a small universe of profound and moving echoes?

With the second verse, Indian writers on poetics, such as Dandin in his Kavyadarsha ('The Mirror of Poetry') would have approved of the insistent alliteration to achieve the same echoes. There are two l's when it comes to the legs, and no less than four f's in the final line, when it comes to frontiers and translucence. By rights the latter ought not to work, but indeed it does, and for whatever inscrutable reason my own flesh bristled with pleasure as I read it...

There is a good reason for such approval. I worked with Karine on her poetry on two occasions, in the summers of 2017 and 2019, both of them on the tiny Greek island of Kythnos. Her commitment to her work is total, so that when her teacher is exhausted by the intensity of the two-way dialogue and dying for coffee, she is always ready for more discussion, and can take or leave the coffee.

As Ernest Hemingway once put it, 'it reads easy cos it's wrote hard'.

John Murray is an English writer. He read Sanskrit at Oxford. He received the Dylan Thomas Award and Lakeland Book of the Year Award. His book Jazz Etc. was longlisted for the Man Booker Prize in 2003.

Part I:
Etchings

The God of Small Things

The History House
"But we can't go in," Chacko explained, "because we've been locked out. And when we look in through the windows, all we see are shadows. And when we try and listen, all we hear is a whispering. And we cannot understand the whispering, because our minds have been invaded by a war. A war that we have won and lost. The very worst sort of war. A war that captures dreams and re-dreams them."
  - Arundhati ROY, 1997

Karine Leno Ancellin

Interview with the Moon

....
Yes! I have, more than once in my life,
suffered the pangs of lack of light
my albedo is not quite right
dark thoughts lurking
I'm not good at emoting!

....
My childhood was seldom joy filled
as my father's rays came to me muddled
my mother, the earth, had so much on her own
that she could not have my needs be known
so I pouted and looked the other way!

....
Not at all, I don't do it on purpose
the tides follow my trajectory, I don't impose,
it's just gravity, I'm only Selene, the sun my master
allays my orbit, his is twice greater
than my inordinate responsibility

....
Not to this day, but I see the useless satellites
every day, whether I'm there or out of sight,
piles of junk orbit with and around me.
What is to happen to all of these debris?
When my proxy life ends,

......
yours will dim, dark.

Karine Leno Ancellin

Nude with Calla Lily, Diego Rivera
To Leno and Paul Sislin

The beige body delineates an ancient clay Amphora
the colour of natural naked arrogance, a nuclear center.

A generous bouquet overflows with white calla lilies
ferociously innocent in their weed-like majestic vanity.

Knees folded under the morphed Lyra's back,
surrendered to the innocent mystery of the lozenge dark

Your open arms orbit these offerings
In a pagan prayer to the glory of Arum Lily life

Each strand of your hair neatly braided
Echoes the woven basket, yet faded

Exposed youth, fragility looking away, vulnerable,
though evanescent in your meditative pose,

A yellow day, the earth dries all desires
ultimate Euridyce sitting, unreachable,

So full of the immanent blessing
give me your sensual flowers for my tomb.

Karine Leno Ancellin

The Missing Angle

Rattleback* Spin

> Venus and I rotate the other way, not wise.
> Other planets rotate on their axes anti-clockwise
> Venus refuses
> I bemuse.

She rotates only clockwise
all to my surprise
there is no 'anti' in her retrograde.

I try, unsuccessful, to find shade
on the wobbly axis I thought myself to belong
it has me mostly wrong.

I am careening through space,
never able to find solace.

> Like my heart swiveling on that kitchen counter
> the counterclockwise deceitful reality
> struggles against all odds,
> for my stubborn clockwise possibility.

*the rattleback is an oblong decorative wooden object from Canada that rotates only one way.

Karine Leno Ancellin

Non-Aligned Love
To Bah

After the 77, love was sold to the market economy,
to 'develop' our sentimental security,
as a corporate construction company.

The couple associates in front of an initiated assembly,
newlyweds are launched on an all inclusive honeymoon,
individuals with numbers they swirl the deal in a ballroom.

A marriage based on basic interests,
each individual believes they own the other,
trading lies, her smile for his 'safety,' the new barter

I have a nomad partner, a part-time husband,
in a different locality, reciprocal felicity,
basked in his tremendous generosity.

Liberty in a couple is a gesture of integrity;
a genuine proof of a project oriented solely,
tenderly to making love with delicacy.

Aesthetics leave the lovers naked.
A volcano, at its core, slopes where affections spree,
far from consumerism inescapability.

Not plans to build an empire,
have children and create a dynasty,
no collective wealth or productivity.

Rather
a commitment to the ecstasy and elegance
of non-alignment and no chosen stance.

Karine Leno Ancellin

The Missing Angle

Art Tandem
To Azzedine and Apolonia

At a post modern duo show, Paris exhibiting,
the wind glued my gaze on an unfinished painting

        two hands, one with a pen and one with a brush
        inspired a monumental love hush

they designed an open avocado, two slices
ONE sole pit, Art its core, its paramount device,

    eyes like the flickering blue-green waters of a Melissani cave
reached across into the sandy Sun-Gilded shine of an infinite desert haze

A love attack, as tenderness sprang out of the canvases,
meandering between guests to find the original dances

        lodged in the ever expanding sphere of this commitment
        to let love sway unto this fiancée agreement

glass in hand, all undulated far and wide in the villa rose
incensed by the heady colors of the musical 'propose'

minimalists conversed in their best theories
hands touched with heightened sensitivities

        time froze, phone and cameras all went blank
        whorled, as in the dizzying quantum of Planck

    Love was to be written
    and painted some more.

Karine Leno Ancellin

Midwifing the Poem
To John Murray

An old Arab Oud sings to the white page
From the oven- sweet and sour spices
colour the creation
feeding my spur with hitches
I rush through the rhythms

Metronome of the word,
the hawk-eye writing master grins.
I have come for an expert appreciation,
meditating on the dismembered motorcycle
outgrown with fresh weeds under the balcony
Romeo traces its own tempo
and I struggle to follow.

The places are assigned,
regal armchair
versus small sitting station
on the side of the couch
with paper and quill in hand, I absorb the advice
awry acerbic and sensitive critique,
as if answers mocked the exercise,

I find the masala mind
peppered hot enough
to climb the sentence,
words ebb on the white page.

Part II:
Virtual Yearnings

In a letter to Lou Andreas Salome, Rilke writes:
"*Songs of longing! And they will resound in my letters, just as they always have, sometimes loudly and sometimes secretly so that you alone can hear them... But they will also be different — different from how they used to be, these songs. For I have turned and found longing at my side, and I have looked into her eyes, and now she leads me with a steady hand.*"
- Rainer Maria Rilke, June 3rd, 1897

Karine Leno Ancellin

Skype Tear
To Ángela

Like the Matisse cut-outs at the MoMa,
your immaterial face, an interface,
as pieces of a puzzle,

Your dried lips blowing a chapped kiss,
your black curls waving the impossibility
to nest in your supple white.

My heart stoops to the moment-
the beats throbbing too loud
for this pixelated slowness.

The virtual frame has caught your eye,
the gold hues of your iris shimmer
shaded by your palm-like lashes...

In a flash,
the dark iris magnified

A tear,
a perfect human tear.

A tear enlarged so real,
I melt as I sit back,

in virtual,
in actual,
ecstasy.

Karine Leno Ancellin

The Missing Angle

iCloud

The sky is filling up the space.
Where is the place where I can forget you?

Chem or con, you trail me... Unsuspected,
between the clouds,
iCloud, meanders thoughts of you

nudging hurdles,
psychology and philosophy,
breaking aloof....

To fly to you
a heart on cloud 9
Desire tight-

stuffing frequencies
and no hertz to flee.

Karine Leno Ancellin

The Missing Angle

buy-ebay
To Stephane

This website is tech perfect.
I'm not following the *Following tab*
just lazily surfing the net on a sunny Sunday afternoon,
perusing through the new age, once in a blue moon

design sophisticates,
color and line syndicates

Ad for a camera –
"In a flash"
Ad for cookie molds –
"culinary cuteness"

'Daily deals for vintage and used'
rainbow letters, I buy
Auction web, founded by Pierre Omidyar
in Teheran, Paris, Baltimore and San Jose.

'Daily deals for vintage and used'
A Marathon,

the deceased's apartment door opens,
the early morning waiting line twists and turns,
first 5 people come in, like a nightclub rush,
buyers tumble in like an avalanche,

post death, it's a mad shove,
frantic frenzied vying, forget love,
the Estate Sale company published the picture,
fight ensues over the Gucci bags lure,

'grab and take' is the rule of the gloom
a company's Cerberus posted in each room,
check the worth on e-bay, then bid
US$100 for the coveted object,
then sell for profit.

Karine Leno Ancellin

The Missing Angle

Antique dealers neglectfully agree,
and saunter to the cashier
run by the estate company,

'Daily deals for vintage and used'
I browse the new objects and
the dealer already has the picture on ebay;

it's a Cartier ring.

Freshly acquired in the morning
off the hand of the deceased.

Karine Leno Ancellin

The Missing Angle

Mood Button

as the screen draws the memory of your touch
facetime admits a fast form of false encounter,

    my skin, erect, reacts to the sting of your pixelated sensuality,
        the curved outline of your Botticelean shoulders,

desperately I hang onto each of your blue jay gray accroche-coeur
sprawled over the too-fluorescent square

    When will I ensconce my lips on your real time- face?

Absorbing the darkness of your light garment,
my gaze ignites mawkish memories.

    My heaving body dances at the mellifluous waking
        your sleepy slit eyes grin at me,
        under feather-soft eyelashes
        shades from the electric light

magnified
an auspicious archaic smile
alluring words
that lull my blood
into an accelerated throb

        Separated
        thousands of
        miles
        a cold bucket
        on the possibility of appeal

All is blocked by the glass cold transparence
listless rendering of our virtual essence.

    I pressed the wrong button and you flashed out
    now I breathe your smoke-tainted frustration.

    The black screen guillotine,

Five thousand miles occupy the reconciliatory kiss.

Karine Leno Ancellin

The Missing Angle

Gmail Novel

Persephone wrote a novel, but it's not published yet.
Thousands of love letters, her romance while it lasted.

re: a zealous exchange, at least six emails each day,
they didn't even need each other's flesh, as they were writing away,
but words wore out. All meanings and connotations experimented,
the concept had waned. It had to be ended.

re: so she left the computer, trying to recompose her being,
the addiction had enslaved her morning routine:
her early woken eyes sleep-walked to the screen
words, impossible to erase, as easy as it seemed.

re: hours she had met with that machine,
sitting, and, typing, and, sighing, and, correcting
each keyboard-letter, emerged of its own accord
laughing its way to the email frame, never bored!

re: the comfortable desk chair now sat cold,
no more fuming tea cups spilled on the desk, hands old,
wasted as if she came from AA, or a night in central park,
the sun had gone out, the keyboard had gone black.

re: all these words lost in the ether: immaterial ideas
imprisoned in the intensity of their letters' follies
she printed them; pale, dead bodies without a casket,
then shredded them into fine strips, score for a foregone minuet

re: the epic conversation still lies on the server
of a heartless corporation,
Warden of the love data, awaiting i-cloud destruction
so she took the strips, assembled them on a canvas

created two fluttering white wings,
dotted in small black print animas.

Karine Leno Ancellin

Late in Love

All these mugs....
I can't tell which one receives your lips?

Having come late in your life,
routines are sealed, inhabited by others.

Only on your being do I feel welcome, each morning anew
– tea-cups trigger oxymoronic sensations,

on the cusp of the cup, my suspicious lips hit ceramic hot
on your exposed skin, my besotted lips lick lukewarm lies

the explored lands of your smitten body give generous hospitality.
unconditionally. To your eyes and mouth, the pull is authentic,

the hurdle is at the gate, martial doormen gossiping,
years of elevators going up or down with the moods of other
loves.

To step in your décor, I must activate the omerta,
become a speck of dust in a China shop, to avoid being crushed.

Because your life was intense, your love so flagrantly immense
it occupies the intangible, the air in the rooms,

the light, the shade, the immaterial DNA,
only your ghost stayed for me.

And I, a post scriptum in your life, I have to live with us thus
find rooms branded, scorched territory,
past of other togethers in nooks and crannies,

I am humble, I don't want to impose,
only to invent love
in this haunted castle.

Karine Leno Ancellin

The Missing Angle

Complex Vortex

Summer is over, and with it, Greece's impromptu felicities.
I quench my need for caring with mechanical duties

*"It's alright if you come to me.
But if you don't it's fine"*

all inspiration in clouds -of- vapors flee,
darn this crash, I hurt   my heart

reeling in   the   manifolds   of   our   i n t r i c a c y

far afield yonder the Atlantic ocean
your mind is replete with phone calls and tasks.

In your far, filled, full agenda, I seek to see priorities
where tenderness would reside, complex vortex

like the lacing marks of mugs on the kitchen counter
plethora of masks, various personae

all   gradually deflate the   wave-frequencies of distance-love

stress swells crescendo mitigated with drudgery,
never allowing any wallowing in sweet nothings,
the gentleness of pillow talk.

Absence is brash when lovers are far,

I am left to commune with the world's wife.

Karine Leno Ancellin

The Missing Angle

Siphoned

Anticipative Greek leaving:
Tongues touch teeth, in an inverted 'tête à tête'
Laughter spills tears in my bloodstream.

Fleeting minutes trek our last communing elation
Too soon, just enough to convert Aegean affection
into transatlantic sufferings. The caryatids wink at your journey.

Time's course will hiccup in your absence.
Books fly in your suitcase, Gurjieff and Rilke
home in New York to home in Athens, do they read the same?

When will you arrive, return, depart and come again?
How will the minutes measure to the dusks and the darks?

Screen reality surrounds you,
salted imbecility flashing out uncouth
how I fear you exposed in this absurdity!

I will hold my moan from the shade of your eyes
clinging to the intensity of your onyx black,
black ink has flurried from my octopus entrails.

My transatlantic tentacles grope for you
and my three hearts buried deep in the crevices of the ocean
anticipate the siphoned bubble in which you will surface.

Karine Leno Ancellin

Soft Stone

My lover left a stone in my hand.

Drumming the beach with her long legs,
veins on marble, lines on limestone,
fine faint frontiers playing on her translucent flesh.

Torso parallel to the horizon line,
she scans the pebbles through sand and weeds
years of practice, her inner radar isolates Millennia marvels.

The eroded lithified orb humbles my pretense
my lover speaks the sediments' rich language,
erring through the rocky scars of time.

She asks each one if they know the Sahara
if it has seen death in the depth of the wine dark sea
she wants to know if sea life is dizzying.

But the stones are not a revealing bunch-
they don't want her to get nosy
so they do it on purpose to hurt her high arch.

Stubborn and inured to life's trials, she persists, seeking
the exclusive clast that will draw a heart-shaped unique pebble,
attesting of the metaphysical narrative-

symbol of our karmic union near the sunbathed sea,
at the bottom lies infinite fright.
Crystal shards lock the sun inside their iridescence.

Does the sacred hurt?
Why do pebbles persist?
Do they really have a choice?
Meanings vacillate on the cusp of the wave.

Are the Greek gods watching our futile efforts
to reconstruct their universe?

My lover said the stone was sentient.

Karine Leno Ancellin

Tangible Melancholy

Does intangibility suffice
to mind-map your absence?

These dark matters of the brain
are where reason collapses.

The misty glow of lamp posts, with their dim light,
swirl cloud ghosts of your silhouette.

All this drizzle, and ardent green lawns, lacking sunbeam,
'Irish Breakfast" socks in a shop window-
an oddity to suit your fine Achilles' ankle.

Eerie skies creep, shutting out light,
It frightens you upon waking.
Every landscape hue howls

your somber scenic shadow.
All the city landmarks emanate old soul,
alone in the unknown land

my guts shrink for lack of oxygen,
there is a glitch in the machine of my body,
its secret mechanisms have gone awry.

Every you construed,
there are so many,
clogged another respiratory channel.

For air, my memory rakes for keepsakes.
Slow cartographer, I delineate,
skin upon skin, appear areas to rename.

Karine Leno Ancellin

The Missing Angle

Scopophilia

A palindrome of visions
outward seeing, inward seen,

Your art-sensitive radar eye,
spots Sapphic shapes on palimpsestes
of hidden Minoan frescoes,

tracking the playful flying swallow
on the high wire against the ochre-crimson sky
canonized by the patience of your Nikkon lens.

Your eye, the verve of your Greek songs,
gleams the language of forlorn myths,
its golden black hues thrill Ymittos shrubs.

Craning in upward movements, aerial reaching.
Your eyes shield swords words,
in a visual assault,
dark and dense mika,
 ready to pulverize.

An enchanted periscope rises from my innermost
to clasp your morphic resonance, in a glance.

Your shooting-eyes wave a shy smile,
I am a switch, you crack on and off <::::

In spite of the expanse,
I dangle on the verdict of your gaze.

Karine Leno Ancellin

Insomnia V

Why is night so different when you lie near me?
I cannot sleep when emptiness mutes your smell
in my vast crisp room, together with roaming jinns,
all kisses gone ~ ~ they do not materialize again,
all the air ~ is free of your ~ smoky ~ breath.

Within the lack of your ~ aura ~ around me
I lay unprotected from lurking nightmares
sardonic Goblins tease my vulnerability,
yonder the pitch dark echoes of fatal red.
Your words have left me expecting the moon to rise eternally ~
in this heterotopic space ~ I lie, unaware of the immensity,
deprived of the book of nothings you whisper in my ear.
No more miracles, your absence is there to stay.

Why is night so different when you lie near me?

Karine Leno Ancellin

Sinister Semester

tear time apart,
it's too trying,
I'm tired...

kiss me, I'm keen,
a lot of space is on me,
even more twirling inside me
now tamed,
stymied for want of tenderness.

Rotten air is all I have,
elections lost and lost again,
I rant, rusty raucous thoughts
absence gnaws freely
in this affection drought

time has lost its pace
it, too, stings
I'm tired...

I hurt, nonsensical and emaciated now,
my blood has diverted its flow
organs erratic, have stopped functioning
nihilist lingering
all stoicism has abandoned me

streets about, creeping
fertile terrain for gangrene
sacrificial burp of last chances,
stop all offerings

time has tread on my authenticity
I go with Estragon, "nothing to be done"
I'm tired.

Karine Leno Ancellin

54

The Missing Angle

From Ares to Eros

Injustices drained me
in an ever-renewed pursuit,
causes kept escaping reality,
adamantly idealist,
possibly pollyannaish,
when tensions escalated into abomination
in remote areas of conflicts,
my naive freedom was muffled
by cringing sounds of oppression.

Dictators were replaced by worse despots
animosity grew between guerilla factions
the Tuareg people never gained a country
the Arab spring reeked in warring volutes
dissolving in the heavy corrupt smolder of oil trade
reinventing themselves in solution-less schisms
that bled my core's deepest throbs,

Until
you unlatched peace,

Until
advocacy shaped the exploration of your metaphysics
conflicts were relegated to their unremitting acrimonies,
outcast in my territory.

My cause, now unique, is nested in your kouros smile
the change in my panoramic imagination swapped surreptitiously
your finely-traced lips swelling,
fluffier amount of kisses,
indifferent to the possibility of war.

Karine Leno Ancellin

The Missing Angle

My metamorphosis went its mysterious path,
serious anxiety soothed away
removed from the proximity of politics
families lost their lives, and my compass dressed in nature's indifference
directing my scrutiny towards the Caryatids' secrets,

my sole advocacy now is to simple love you in your country stream,
who am I betraying?

Part III:
Accents of Myths

"It's all been an experience of inbetweenness –neither here nor there, the usual globalization stuff really- however, I would rather call it a here-and-there-ness, not being in between but being in both places at once, with the added difficulty that these are not real, objective, "out there" places after all. Both East and West are provinces of the mind."

Orfeas Apergis, March 12, 2019
About his book, 'Their Tongue' ('Η γλώσσα τους'), in Greek News Agenda

Karine Leno Ancellin

The Missing Angle

Odysseas

I know of him,
> and of his sorrows,

his pains at sea, leaving captivity seven years thence,
> like mine at love, expecting the end of torture and violence

Under the aegis of Athena, he survived and suffered
> with my guardian angels I resist, hung on to the undecided

land ahoy, he drifted to the bottom of the rocky cliffs
> as I drowned in the spasms of passionate riffs

he did not see the breach to reach land or beach
> angry waters lick me, I screech

he divests Calypso's toga on the boulders emerged
> estranged, I look to retrace the glory that Love erected

the divine tows him, mortal with no life, to shore and beauty
> like the sky allows sun rays, when metamorphosis hiccups I agree

Karine Leno Ancellin

The Missing Angle

left as an algae uprooted from its seafloor bush, dried up on the shore,

    I lack sap, in this parched loveloss land,

He lay bare under the gaze of naked Nausicaa and maid.

    I chance Serendip will allow gravity, my love murmured.

Karine Leno Ancellin

Free Fall

Dressed in black, not ostensibly anarchist
A bear hug type of young man, Gregory
one more mythic Greek motorist....

The dark hair of ancient Athenians
an average Apollo with alternating beard lengths

coffee and cigarettes.
His girlfriend, Vassiliki,
behind the wheel,
in love,

Until this night of September, *"the day I'll always remember"*
when he headed
    from the balcony
    to his death
        below

His mother in disbelief,
Vassiliki was looking for her shoes and keys.

He went past, so fast,
a few steps along the couch of kisses
by the fireplace in the living room,
his crazed gaze,
fatal home, he was born in,
    all was familiar,
        except death

                that day
            he had erased all traces
        deleted his blog off the internet

Like the untouchables
sweeping away their steps……
....
no more words……………….
....

Karine Leno Ancellin

The Missing Angle

....
he subtracted his 'self'...........

kanenas –had- traveled,
opened the caches where life was hidden
alongside his captain father,
in Brazil he thought of 'other ways'
the *"permitted way"* he argued, "*that's all you see,*"

        he was 'other'
        too much responsibility, yet still an anarchist

I was too busy, I didn't call him back,
guilt, f****, pain further than fear,
iF I had..................if,   IF   IF F F* F F F Fly
                                                in search of absolute

Outside Athens' main jail,, at Christmas,
he yelled sweet words to cheer the prisoners,
forever protesting, against the trials of innocents.

He came to me as a Greek mentor, an immaterial gift
from Cavafy, The Master and Margarita, Nietszche,
generous,

above all, in the void he left,
I see:

an ocean of ugly greed
....
no words...........................
....

...........Ο Γρήγορης ..."*write it with 2 itas*"
"yes, it's a feminine vowel" he smiled,

        Orphaned,
your words,
glue to our minds.

Karine Leno Ancellin

Exile in Frantic Folly
To Alaa and Ruda

In the hands of smugglers
preying on their savings,
and their beauty
these humans are innocent of the history
of the mythical West they fled to.

Years of callous colonization, pillaging and local divisions
have secured Superman's white confidence.

The lucky ones that flee will fill
that layer of tedious jobs no one else wants,
disregarding their skills.
They have left everything behind.

Indifference is easy, like Pontius Pilates' sense of responsibility,
tribal feuds led people here, to Greece, within the diameter of the
Pnyx.

The archaic irony of the kouroi smile.

In long milli-seconds, bombs, planes, gases, shots, panic
all abandoned
families
friends,
homes,
land,
language
affections.

Karine Leno Ancellin

Pireas Welcome

Desperately seeking dignity
at the Greek Port of Pireas.

Grey, drizzly, wet winds wash the Pier E1.
Never on Sunday at the port of Pireas,
like somber and slippery Parian marmoreal,
catharsis for confused hopes and hates
are enmeshed in a void-filled horizon.

Flashes of trauma inset in daily routines,
part of the fabric of exilic souls.

Clouds of conflicts
hide the Greek sun from a slow sky,
water drips on the cement,
MSF attempting a last medical chance
zillions of sleazy raindrops....
pluck.. pluck ...pluck... liquid sorrow
in damp and sly spates, too light to be feared,
surreptitious torture.

Pireas is agitated by a humongous sense of loss
when this end of the tether is reached,
it's the 'grab and take' intuit, 'nothing more to lose' at Pier E1
The fringe territory of Athens' homeless,
with more homeless than them.

Greek trucks unloading, Spanish volunteers ferrying.
Thanks to the Athenians, basic sustenance is possible
emaciated faces, chaotic food distribution,
mounds of bread from the capital's denizens.

Hunger tenses, legs rush by as the
magnitude,
in despair,
is engulfing foreign goodwill.

Karine Leno Ancellin

The Missing Angle

The human condition is violent,
frustrated, malevolent, loud, lured, lewd,

purple clouds incessantly pouring more privations-
even poverty is a luxury!

No monuments will be erected on Pier E1

Karine Leno Ancellin

The Missing Angle

Racked Refugees
To Maya

Like the winged Victory of Samothrace
standing uprooted in the Louvre today.
Like the ruins of Athens' statues,
displayed for all to admire.

it is the head that goes first,
the head that breaks away from the body
the head, that the erosion
of water currents cuts off.

Drowned refugees bodies land awash
on the beach of Tunisia, in Zarzis.
A cherub body without a head,
an ancient Athenian ruin, still wet.

In the Acropolis museum
statues have lived through centuries
without their extremities,
still retaining their exquisite misery

in the cemetery of Unknown,
Chemseddine Marzoug has buried
dismembered parts of subhuman hope
racked in the milk of human cruelty.

Karine Leno Ancellin

Athena's Blaze
Dedicated to Panos Kokkinidis and family

Amongst Athens' top pastry chefs,
Panos Kokkinidis
was spending a warm summer day near Mati,
a picturesque beach town, suave and lovely,
on the Aegean shore of Greece.

He had mastered the art of fire,
crafting innovational delicacies,
well-known with the Athenian literati.

So when the grey flames came blazing towards
him, his wife, his children and his mother,
he took his phone out and began filming
not knowing what he could be expecting,
he posted the agonizing video,
struck by this monumental inferno.
A slithering colossal amber moving
like an incandescent dragon approaching
denser and closer
scorching the children and elderly first
threatened and afraid,
all scampered, fast
the somber smoke asphyxiating first
as the diabolical flares
crawled black into their flesh.
All dead.

Panos perished-
a burning man,
the flames had devoured their master.

Karine Leno Ancellin

The Missing Angle

A plastic dumpster melted in its own carcass,
the fire had gone on a Daliesque rage.
Scattered- burnt doors still in fumes,
carbonized, peeled cables
much like macabre carnations,
sardonic skeletons of electric, metal boxes
dangled on worn-out weeping walls
their imperial power annihilated,
a waste of human sacrifice.

The tranquil blue now nags at the blanket of silver ash-dust,
why is its turquoise so arrogant, so indifferent?
Is there no suffering in this crystal sea?

The fire had devastated the lands
leaving nothing to soothe the empty hands

Death was irrevocable,
nothing to hang on to for rebirth,
not a thing left not turned to ashes.

Karine Leno Ancellin

The Missing Angle

On the Wall Stood a Picture

On a greige suede wall stood a picture
of Tuareg refugees resting in the shade, on a straw mat
under a flimsy tree, with bundles of stuff they salvaged
folded in haste fleeing from the Malian military.

Refugee camp stories of rape, shootings, and death,
lodged bats in the cave of their minds.
Lifted veils show inerasable wounds while
malnourished children whine around

family members missing,
unrelenting hope
with the grace of the same god
who had overseen them ending up in this forsaken place.
A chaos of love schlepped with a few tin pans!

Desolation miniaturized on a New York City greige suede wall
cozily looking out onto the east river stroll
occupants oblivious to this scene,
displayed as an antique meme.

Twenty years later, the Tuareg people are probably alive
in northern Mali, still suffering from clanic rivalry.
Two improbable worlds contained haphazardly
at the extreme of our planet's polarity

the simple smiles in that picture
ordinary wisdom
in the ever-wanting,
ever-seeking New York City art scene.

Karine Leno Ancellin

The Missing Angle

Fluid Dawn

from the obscure depths of melancholy,
I silently emerge to swirling seagulls in the skies of New York City
on a pale and sincere blue dawn, neglecting its golden raiment

the Yemeni chest progressively comes back into place,
grief has followed chaos. In this space

I lay by the couch-window, surrendered to the slow, soft soreness
cars hum their fast and busy agenda, on the Koch bridge traffic stress
while I challenge the finite which has broken my breath in before and after

the frozen river has lost its treacherous appeal
to fall through its luring thin, white layer congealed

the dark, golden-brown of Aphrodite I had dreamt before birth
glows sincerity at me, I read the non-defined semantic inside,
her features reveal a spatial voyage within this tight time alive

together we glide into the meanders
of this non-threatening, non-delineated, anonymity

my blurred femininity draws on the blossoming Vergissmeinnicht*
tracing into the legend of Androgyny

Paris, Athens or New York,
birds always awaken to Shams at dawn

*Myosotis scorpioides (forget-me-not flower)

Karine Leno Ancellin

The Missing Angle

In-divi-dual

The mind functions in the color of its tongue
mine is cognitive dissonance
one time American, one time French,
also referencing Arabic and Greek,
without rhyme or reason.

My brain separates representations
pain in English is further encroaching than pain in French
although, I learned pain was originally wounded in French.
Does it make a difference if my rant
is spelled in one tongue or another,
without rhyme or heart sway?

Already I found my way out of the collective
The tribal chants cringed–IN- my soul
singularity screamed from my –DIVI- ded
upbringing, with –DUAL- references
I could not coordinate with geographic models
without rhyme or country.

I was the jarring note in national orchestras,
my sense of rhythm was flawed
a glitch in the natural sense of belonging;
words meant other tunes
without rhyme or melody.

Comfortably settled in one's mother tongue
the other barged in unpredictably, forcing entry

then I found hospitality in mythologies.

Karine Leno Ancellin

Pathetic Pragmatism

Beloved Greece, why is poetry so delightful?
Are you becoming forgetful?
When did you satisfy aesthetics with a bellyful?
Did Sappho write about her schedule?

Pathetic pragmatism, a false premise,
"Did you service the car last week?"
"Why can't we go shopping now?"
Carry the groceries.
Know what you need to buy.
Buy and stock,
a hoarding malady
practical greed,
a pathology.

Useful is anathema to Poetry,
a moment's acumen magnified.

I leave the table...
get away from the company,
to check if my hair is tucked properly.
The eclipse,
it revived my vision.
I re-see another spectacle of the same invitation.

My heart is deep at bay.
The pragmatic offends my day.
My moon is procrastinating months away.
I go astray.

Part IV:
Epilogue

The Missing Angle

Mooted

Greece handed me
what I didn't know
I was missing
everything I had been entitled to,
and bereft of,
a mythology to face the travails of the day
a home with a poetic room of my own.

Like the nymphs of mount Olympus
I had longed to become myself
after the devoted wife and mother
after the journalist,
passionate with unjust causes
after the literature professor,
hidden behind torrents of words
in shame, guilty of what I was lacking
as a naiad, embarrassed
I aspired to poetry.

In places:
from America, to Africa, to Europe's diversity,
I had tried to belong-
to find osmosis or serenity,
and like a foreign graft
it was eventually rejected.

Greece bestowed, xenophilia
a life examined, mine,
I discovered my ancestral Home,
dryad, I stayed and I nested,
grew "roots and safety"
my vital delicacies.

Appreciated,
not for how graciously I endured
not for how genuinely I reported
not for my "excuse-me" generosity,

Karine Leno Ancellin

The Missing Angle

more for,
a curiously wandering mind,
an intrinsic evolutionary activism
for being innately creative,

a mentor of dreams,
wrapped in woman's flesh,
another Athenian ruin.

A Note on Coffee Grinds

I read the coffee grinds as poems: not as telling the future, but instead as a special and intricate narrative to whom one has surrendered their deepest intimacy. Thus, these coffee images are a confessional Mise en Abyme of my poems. Like the coffee reader, I am a scarred intercessor between my crooked reality and my crooked words. There is an initiation: it is a mystique one enters, like a stream of consciousness. Coffee grind readings, like the other forms of divination I studied, are part of the insignificant poetic pacts that one seals with the ordinary - an aesthetic grace bestowed on human interactions. As with the poetry, they are hummed tunes innate to our quotidian.

A SINGULAR MUSE
an afterword by Lee Slonimsky

When reading for the first time the exquisitely original and adroit poems of Karine Ancellin, the reader is immediately inspired to cast about in her or his memory of poetry for a precedent.

Wonderful internal rhymes like "space" and "solace" (in "Rattleback* spin"); memorable syntax like "I dangle on the verdict of your gaze" (in "Scopophilia"); and striking alliteration like "I rant, rusty raucous thoughts" (in "Sinister Semester") are just a few examples of the singular in Ancellin's poetry, compelling moments that make the reader feel fortunate to be discovering such unique work.

Many of these poems can be characterized as love poems, hardly the first time this topic has been addressed in poetry, but love poems with a memorable phrase, a fine detail, a beautiful image that make love as fresh and new as it has ever been. "Soft Stone" is a most innovative affirmation of her feelings for the one she loves, yet also makes direct reference to the deep Homeric tradition behind all the world's poetry: "She asks each one if they know the Sahara/if it has seen death in the depth of the wine dark sea.../symbol of our karmic union near the sunbathed sea;" "wine dark sea" of course referring back to *The Odyssey*. Ancellin's love comes across in this unforgettable poem as a poet too, even a prophetess who finds sentience in a stone.

Other poems more broadly characterize modern life, in Greece for one example: "Pathetic Pragmatism" includes the memorable and wistful observation, "Did Sappho write about her schedule?" This poem brings ironic observation to an art form in itself! In general, across the pages, the range of subject, beauty, insight and wisdom dazzles.

After considerable reflection, one earlier poet comes to mind who resembles Ancellin in certain aspects of her work, such as the offhand, compelling observation; the engaging and intimate flow of words. That poet is Frank O'Hara, famous participant in the "New York School" of poetry from several decades ago. A brief excerpt from the O'Hara poem "Portrait" ("my lilies, your powders/upon the smoky air/while glassy eyes pursue their indifferent way") gives a sense of the dynamic verve that characterizes Ancelline's luminescent poems as well, light-filled as they are with deep observation and exceptional wit.

But even the O'Hara comparison, intriguing as it is, does not do justice to the scope and intensity of these marvelous poems. *The Missing Angle* is a book of discovery, a unique voice accessible and moving to anyone who has the thrill of reading it for the first time, or again and again.

Lee Slonimsky is a poet, "Pythagorean" scholar and a polymath. He is the author of nine collections of poetry and co-author with Carol Goodman, his wife and Hammett Prize novelist, of The Black Swan Rising trilogy (under the name Lee Carroll) and other novels. Amongst his books of poetry are Talk Between Leaf and Skin (2002), Pythagoras in Love, (2007). Logician of the Wind (2012). Lion, Gnat, (2017).

Photograph by Angela Lyras

About the Author

Karine Leno Ancellin was born and grew up in New York until she moved to different countries. She researched 'Hybrid identities' for her Phd at the Vrije Universiteit of Brussels having earned an MA, with Honors, in Comparative Literature at the Charles V Institute of Paris VII. She worked as a journalist in West Africa for many years and currently is a professor, writer and translator living in Athens, Greece. Along her poetry writing, Karine Ancellin has now turned to literary journalism and publishes free-lance. She is also involved in the promotion of pan-Hellenic Literature and co-founded a poetry society in Athens, Greece with Angela Lyras (www.apoetsagora.com). Some of her poems have been put to jazz music by the composer Leila Olivesi.

Acknowledgements

Very many thanks to all those who helped me in so many different ways to understand that my words could matter. First, I would like to address my warm gratitude to Ava Balis, my Publisher and Beth Huston, my editor for their kindness and patience. Secondly, I also want to thank the people who inspired and nurtured my imagination, such as my mentors whose words are included here and Katerina Anghelaki-Rooke. Amongst my friends those who either read my manuscripts or encouraged my work along its long path are Sabeen Thomson, Daniele Lamarche, Hannah Beresford, Anna Klebnikov and Columbia Prof. Arcadi Nebolsine, Stephane Pantano, Delphine Sdika Singh, Amel Daddah, Xristina Moschaki, Mihalis Montesantos, Muepu Mwamba, Nancy Hooff and Jim Campbell, my ex-husband Bah Saleck, Agnes Deshormes and Pierre Baris who often extended a writing space in their beautiful home in Paris. Most of all, I want to thank my sons whose love nourish my life's drive in multitude of ways. And last and particularly important, I want to express gratitude to Leno and Paul Sislin whose encouragement of my writing has been unwavering for a long long time. Another pillar of strong support, in every step of the process, that I would like to warmly thank here is Angela Lyras for her constant and renewed trust in my creativity.

I would also like to thank these magazines and presses for giving homes to versions of the poems in this manuscript:

'Mooted' in the Anthology 'Curating Alexandria', February 2019
'Late in Love'/ International Poetry Digest, May 2019 edition
'Skype Tear'/ Silver Stork Magazine / Issue FLUX 2018
'Skype Tear' was used by Jazz composer Leila Olivesi for her last album, 'Suite Andamane.'
'Athena's blaze' / Moon Magazine / January 2019;
'Racked Refugees' - 'Icloud' - 'Interview with the Moon'/Active Muse Magazine 2019
'Odysseas' / Hive Avenue Literary Journal / March 2019;
'Free Fall' was in performance by the author at the Prithvi Theatre, Mumbai, India, In Memoriam.
'Mood Button' / Riza Press Multimedia Poetry and Art Journal / 2019

This selection of poems is also a tribute in gratitude for the kindness and openness of the contemporary Greek poets I am involved with via my Athenian poetry society, A Poets' Agora. www.apoetsagora.com